MW01058133

A Week Or Two In The Canadian Rockies

Rockies

What to see and do in two weeks or less

By Darren Critchley

Table of Contents

Why You Need To Read This Book

There is so much to see and do in the Canadian Rockies that it can be very overwhelming. The goal of this book is to try to help you plan up to a two week long stay in the Canadian Rockies. Many tourists planning to visit the Rockies do so armed only with a brochure or magazine and hope for the best. They do not take into account the distance between attractions, the season, the weather and the other tourists when planning a trip. I am going to try to help you pick the best time to go, the best time to visit places and help you organize it into a reasonable order. I am going to break down the sections of the Rockies into manageable areas that you can then explore all the options presented and get the most out of your time. Using the towns of Banff, Lake Louise, Jasper and the Icefields Center as bases to stay at, I have put together a list of the attractions for each area. Each of these lists will tell you how many days (or hours) it will require to see the attractions. You can mix and match these attractions to make out an itinerary that works best for you. Because I do not know which direction you are coming from, it makes it very difficult to make a one size fits all itinerary.

In this book I will be focusing on the Yoho, Banff and Jasper National parks, which include the towns of Field, Lake Louise, Banff, and Jasper. There is another National Park in the Rockies called Kootenay National Park, it is in the southern part of the Rockies and I will be covering that part of the Rockies in a future book.

While this book is aimed primarily at tourists who are traveling in recreational vehicles, it will work equally well for tourists staying in hotels, as there is a hotel located in every place I mention in this book. I have always traveled the Rockies in a recreational vehicle and therefore, bookings and information will be focused on RV's, but each National Park site, under where to stay will mention the hotels or other accommodations available – sorry, I just don't have the information to tell you about hotels, I prefer to camp in the Canadian Rockies.

Darren Critchley

Introduction

My name is Darren Critchley and I have been visiting the Canadian Rockies since I was a small child. I try to visit them every year and stay for at least a week. In my visits to the Rockies, I always try to find something new to explore, and usually do. There is just so much to see and do, even after visiting for a lifetime, I am still pleasantly surprised to find new things. I live in Vernon, British Columbia about five hours west of the Canadian Rockies, and usually come to the Rockies from the west into Jasper or Lake Louise.

I also camp elsewhere throughout British Columbia and Alberta and run into many tourists that are heading into the Rockies. Many of these tourists are from Europe or the United States and have flown into Calgary or Vancouver, then rented an RV and headed off to the Rockies for a week or two. It is these people that prompted me to write this book. They all have one thing in common, they want to see the Rockies and expect it to be a quick and easy trip because somewhere, some travel agent has sold them a package. So off they head into the Rockies, armed only with a list of private campsites that are partners to the rental company and a few tourist brochures. I have run into these tourists as early as mid April and I can tell you that April through June can be a very miserable time in the Canadian Rockies. Actually, in April and a lot of May, you will run into snow. Of course the travel agent never informs them about the weather, just that the crowds will be a lot less at this time of the year. Nor the facts that many attractions and campsites are not even open that early.

So it is my intent to hopefully correct some of this misinformation and help inform those that are planning a trip to the Rockies. With that in mind, let us get on with the book . . .

Darren Critchley

Section One - A Little Planning And Consideration Before You Go

Chapter One - The Weather

The weather in the Rockies is temperamental to say the least. It can change at a moment's notice, even in the middle of summer, which is a very short season by the way. Most of the towns and places you will visit in the Rockies are over 5000 feet (1524 meters) above sea level. That is pretty high, in fact Lake Louise Village is the highest community in Canada at 5052 feet (1540 meters), the actual lake and Chateau itself is even higher than that.

At this altitude, weather comes in fast and changes rapidly, even in the middle of summer. Not to frighten you, but you have to be aware of the weather and plan accordingly, particularly if you like hiking. I remember a few years back we were hiking up to the top of Fairview Mountain, a 9,002 foot (2744 meter) peak right next to Lake Louise, we had about 500 feet (152.4 meters) to go and had to make a decision on whether or not to turn back because a storm was coming in from the southeast. Fortunately it never reached us, as we were ill prepared that day for a storm. The weather down below was above 68°F (20°C) and sunny. A lesson learned on being properly prepared.

So regardless of when you go, the weather is going to be a huge factor, even ruining some parts of your trip. The best you can do is to try to minimize the effects of weather by choosing one of the better times of the year to visit and also plan indoor or town based activities if the weather gets miserable. I should also mention here that temperature is also a factor in the Rockies, it can get downright cold! I have been in the Rockies where the temperature has been as high as 96.8°F (36°C) during the day and dropped to just above freezing at night on the same day! Again, you are pretty high up and that really affects the temperature.

In all honesty, the best time to plan your trip to the Rockies is actually August (the later the better) – the absolute busiest time in the

Rockies. Late July and early September would be a close second, particularly early September if the weather has been good throughout August – the only thing is that the interpretative shows have shut down in the National Parks and things are on a wind down. I personally prefer to deal with the crowds in sunny weather than to have it quieter and with inclement weather. I have traveled the Rockies in April, June, July, August and September and stick to my guns, late August, while busier, is the best weather. I've been driven out of the Rockies in late June and the second week of July by snow, it does happen and it is not much fun! You will also find that until the month of May, many of the attractions, museums, and some of the campsites will not be open.

As a side note, as I am writing this, it is the first week of June 2012 and the Lake Louise campground is completely closed and the city of Banff is erecting barriers of sand bags because the Bow River has flooded its banks. Due to a large snow pack last winter and a quick thaw this spring, rivers throughout Canada are overflowing their banks. The Canadian Rockies is no different. Weather does play a huge role in your trip, and one should try to have contingency plans in case an attraction is closed.

Chapter Two - Booking Your Campsites

As I said in the last chapter, I think the best time to go is late August, which is also the busiest time in the Rockies, but with some planning and some reservations, you can make it work for you.

I never go to the Rockies anymore without my campsite booked ahead of time (at least since Parks Canada came out with the reservation system). Once you know when and where you are going to in the Rockies, I would highly recommend contacting Parks Canada via their website (*http://www.pccamping.ca*) or their toll free number (1-877-737-3783) or outside of North America (1-450-505-8302) to make your reservations. You will need a credit card handy and will need to know what kind of recreational vehicle you will be using, as well as its length. There are still some spots where you cannot reserve, which is the smaller campsites that can be found away from the towns, these are on a first come, first serve basis and require a bit of forethought on planning.

Pricing for the campsites can be found online at the Parks Canada website *http://www.pc.gc.ca* Click on Find a National Park from the left hand side. Then enter the name of the National Park, ie) Banff. Click on the link to the park from the search results. Next click on visitor information in the left hand side. Then click on where to stay. Next click on the campgrounds link. Finally you will be presented with a list of campgrounds within the national park you chose (phew, a lot of work if I do say so myself). After you read the rules (and all the regulations on the consumption and possession of alcohol) there is a table with each campsite listed, the types of sites, the cost, and when it is open. NOTE: before May, many of the campsites are not open, only a select few are open through what is considered the winter months, so PLEASE make sure the campground you are going to is open. Also of note, the reservation site is a different web address than the main Parks Canada website.

The online reservation system is great, it allows you to choose the type, size and options for your campsite. There are different kinds of campsites throughout the national parks and even within the same campsite. For example, in Jasper, at Whistlers campsite, you can

3

choose one of the following types of campsites, one with a fire pit, one with electricity & sewer, and one with electricity & a fire pit.

If you use the online reservation system, make sure you print out the piece of paper with the bar code on it. It simplifies your check in when you get to the campsite, which depending upon the time of day and where you are at, checking in can be a lengthy experience. Also, before you go, write down the address for the Parks Canada website as well as their phone numbers, these can come in handy for making changes during your trip.

For myself, when I go to the Rockies, I usually just reserve the first leg of the trip, which is usually the busiest and most important part of the trip – typically Lake Louise, we are partial to the tenting section, it has a nice electrified fence around it, which makes me a little more comfortable with the kids. Once we leave Lake Louise, we either show up at other campsites and hope for a decent spot, or go online again and book them. You can also go into the Parks Canada office and book in person. There are Parks Canada offices located in the town of Jasper, the town of Banff and the village of Lake Louise. This has worked well for us for years, with the exception of Jasper, it seems either we have horrible luck or the weather is always bad out there. In the umpteen visits to Jasper, two of them have been sunny and clear, it took me five trips with my own family before I was able to get them up the tramway, and then because of forest fires the view was spoiled! We always leave Jasper as an open-ended trip; we'll stay a day or so and move on if it is miserable.

One final note, you cannot reserve a campsite on the same day you are arriving at the campsite, so unfortunately you need to know what you are doing at least a full day ahead of time.

Chapter Three - When To Arrive At Your Campsite

This depends entirely on the time of year you are taking your trip, with July and August being the busiest. The rest of the time, there is not a lot to worry about, but in summer, these places, particularly Lake Louise and Jasper get very busy. Line-ups to get into the campgrounds are long, even with reservations, there is no express lane for reservations, which is a shame, there should be in places like Lake Louise and Whistlers in Jasper (take note Parks Canada).

According to the Parks Canada website, check in time for reservations is 2PM, however, I have found through past experience that about an hour after check out, your spot should be available. Check out time is 11 am, and shortly thereafter is a great time to arrive at most of the campsites. Depending upon the person working the kiosk, some will wait a full hour after checkout before deeming a spot available, so sometimes a spot may not be available to you until after 12pm, particularly if you choose one of the limited spots such as power. The majority of spots in the campgrounds are unserviced.

Also, try not to arrive late, I found through experience that the reservation system falls apart when you arrive late. I remember one year we had reserved two spots in Jasper with fire pits, but had experienced some vehicle trouble on our way up and arrived after 5PM. When we handed the reservation sheet in, we were given spots without fire pits at which time I complained and they just said, too bad, you were late. So be very careful about arriving late in these campsites, otherwise you could meet with disappointment. If you have reserved, you will always get a spot, but it may not be the one you wanted. Also, their cancellation policy is not a friendly one, if you fail to show up, you can pretty much kiss your money goodbye, particularly if you are only staying for one night.

Darren Critchley

Chapter Four - Park Fees

Yes, there are Park Fees associated with visiting the National Parks; these fees pay for maintenance, upgrades, policing, staff, sanitation and a ton of other things necessary to keep a National Park running.

Current fees for each park (pretty much the same across the board), can be found by going to the Parks Canada website (*http://www.pc.gc.ca*) clicking on Fees in the left hand column (in the Explore category), then click on the green bar that says "Current List of Fees > Search". Enter the park you are going to be in, such as Banff. Click on the National Park listed under National Parks that you were searching for. A list of fees for being in the park will come up, as well as camping fees.

Now, every visitor to a National Park, if they stop in the Park, are required to have a National Park Pass. You can purchase these passes at any Parks Canada office, or kiosk. There are varying prices for the entry passes depending upon whether or not you are a senior, youth, family, or individual. If your group has seven or less people and are all traveling in the same vehicle, then you can purchase the family pass. In the past, I have found that for most people, the family pass is the best value and if you are staying more than seven days in the National Park system, then the Annual Family Pass is the best value. The same applies for each category of visitor, you will have to look at the pass prices and work out the best one for your situation. But make sure you purchase a pass once you are in the park system, as they are required to enter the campgrounds, and they will make you buy one at the gate, which might put you on the spot. The same also applies for some of the highways going through the National Parks, there are entry kiosks that check for passes on both ends of the Icefields Parkway, as well as the East entrance to Banff National Park.

If you reserve a campsite with a firepit and wish to have a fire, there is an extra fee for a fire permit. However, this includes your firewood.

There are two National Historic Sites located in Banff National Park and one in Glacier National Park (about 3 hours southwest of Banff National Park). If you plan on visiting any of these National Historic Sites, then you will be required to pay a further fee to Parks Canada for entrance to the sites. I will cover these sites in detail further in the book, but suffice to say they are worth visiting, particularly the two in Banff. The only reason I mention this here is that there is an annual pass available (as well as a family pass) that it may be more beneficial to purchase an annual pass depending upon the size of your group.

Finally the only other fee that we have not covered is the one for fishing! Yes, there is a fee for that too, which can be found on the same page as all the other fees from the web address I posted earlier in this section. The fishing permit is available in Daily or Annual and depending upon your length of stay and number of days you fish, it can be more beneficial to purchase the annual one. Note: the fishing permit is ONLY valid in the National Park, once you leave the National Park System, you are subject to the Conservation laws of either Alberta or British Columbia and you can check their respective websites for permit information. The link for Alberta is *http://www.albertaregulations.ca/fishingregs/* and British Columbia can be found here *http://www.env.gov.bc.ca/fw/fish/regulations/* If you plan on fishing on your trip, please insure you have the proper permit to do so, both Provincial Governments and the National Parks enforce the regulations and the penalties are stiff.

Chapter Five - What Kind Of Clothing To Bring

Basically you need to bring enough clothing to cover a varied set of conditions, as I mentioned in the first chapter about weather. The weather can change in an instant in the Rockies. In summer, temperatures can get as high as 96.8°F (36°C) and at the same time, can cool off to just above freezing at night. Your best bet is to layer your clothing (and rain gear) so that you can take off what you don't need and put it back on when necessary. While it is beyond the scope of this book to tell you what exactly you need to wear, I will say you should have the following essentials to enjoy your trip. Number one, bring an umbrella, you never know when you will need it. Bring some sort of light rainwear as well. For your feet bring some sturdy footwear and hiking books if you plan on doing a lot of hiking. A toque and gloves would not go amiss as well, I can remember several times sitting around the fire in August with toques on our heads!

As for planning ahead, I can remember one time in Jasper where it was raining beyond belief, we had no umbrellas and were going from store to store to try to purchase some. When you are in the Rockies, most stores accommodate the tourists and their prices are set accordingly – plan ahead.

Darren Critchley

Chapter Six - Wildlife

Finally, I want to talk a little about wildlife. When you enter the Rocky Mountain Parks, you will be in some of the most pristine forests you will ever come across. It is a protected environment and for a good reason, there is a ton of wildlife here. The wildlife within Park boundaries is all protected by the National Parks Act, which means don't interfere with it and definitely do not feed it! As tempted, as you are to feed that bird, squirrel or hairy marmot, please don't, they will die from human food. On top of that, it teaches them to be reliant upon humans for food and they will lose their fear of humans, which will eventually lead to their having to be destroyed.

Throughout all the National Parks, you will encounter wildlife pretty much everywhere, including in the towns. It is not uncommon to see Caribou or Elk strolling through one of the towns in the National Parks. These are wild animals, and even though they are in what appears to be an urban environment, please give them a wide berth. Take pictures, but stay back and be cautious. Parks Canada says for an elk or deer keep back at least three bus lengths. For bears, cougar or wolf, they suggest at least ten bus lengths.

Be aware in your campsite as well, with the exception of Lake Louise tenting area, wildlife (bears, caribou, elk, moose) can all come walking through your campsite. You need to be aware of this and avoid attracting them to your campsite. Parks Canada is very strict on what you can leave unattended around your campsite. For example coolers and food left outside your RV are a big no, no. In fact, they will confiscate your cooler and you have to drive up to the office to get it back. Do it more than once and they will show you the door, or the exit to the campground.

You will also encounter wildlife while driving down the highway, it is very easy to spot in the National Parks, it is where the traffic has completely come to a stop and a bunch of cars, buses and RV's are apparently parking. If you come across this (and you will), do not be tempted to leave your vehicle as so many do, you are endangering your life, as well as the wildlife. Too many times I have seen people rushing down embankments to get a picture of that Grizzly bear with her cubs, not realizing that if you get too close, that Grizzly will protect its offspring. I'm not trying to scare you here, just want you to realize that the wildlife is, well, wild and to be respected. If you leave it alone, it will leave you alone. By all means get your picture, which is why we are here, but stay well back; all of today's cameras have excellent zoom features.

Chapter Seven - Where To Camp and Why

There are three main places I stay when going to the Rockies, which I kind of call base camps and one in between spot in the Columbia Icefields. From each of these sites you can pretty much be within an hour or less of all of the sights that one would want to see. I am by no means advocating that you only stay in these spots, but it makes it a lot easier on reservations, and traveling when you stick to them. There are of course lots of other campgrounds within the park boundaries, check the Parks Canada website for more information. So that is the "**Why**" part of where to camp and now onto the where.

I am going to list off each of these places and tell you the distance from a major city and driving time between them, this should help you plan out your days when moving between them. Remember, all times are if you are driving straight through, there are lots of pull offs and scenery to see on these routes and it can take much longer to make the trip. In fact if you stopped at every pull off to view the scenery, it would take a significantly much longer time to get to your destination. I have however, included the usual time it takes to view or hike an attraction, to help you plan your trip.

Jasper, Alberta

I'll start with Jasper, which is at the north end of the Icefields Parkway.
Jasper is located 273 miles (439 kilometers) northeast of Kamloops, British Columbia and 227 miles (366 kilometers) southwest of Edmonton Alberta on Highway 16. To the south via the Icefields Parkway (Hwy 93) is Lake Louise, Alberta, which is 141 miles (227 kilometers), approximately 3.5 hours driving time without stopping to view the sites. If you are not coming from central British Columbia or Northern Alberta, then Jasper will be a side trip from Lake Louise, one that is very worthwhile. Jasper has several extremely large campgrounds as well as many hotels, cottages, cabins and bed & breakfasts. The town of Jasper is actually located within the National Park. Jasper also has several grocery stores, a hospital, several gas

stations, laundry facilities as well as lots of restaurants. There are multiple automated bank machines available here as well as some banks. When staying in Jasper, I always try for the Whistlers campground, mainly because it has pull through sites with power and fire pits. That means that if it rains, the kids can still watch a movie and be out of our hair. On my last trip in 2011, I was late in reserving our campsite and ended up in Wapiti, with just a fire pit, Whistlers was completely full!

Lake Louise, Alberta

Lake Louise is located just inside the British Columbia/Alberta border on the Trans Canada Highway. It is 272 miles (437 kilometers) east of Kamloops, British Columbia and 34.2 miles (55 kilometers) west of Banff, Alberta. It is approximately an hour from Banff and 3.5 hours from Jasper. Lake Louise has one large campground. There are numerous hotels, motels, cabins, cottages and bed & breakfasts in Lake Louise. Lake Louise is a tiny community that has one small strip mall containing a liquor store, post office, candy shop, bakery, grocery store, bookstore, several souvenir shops and a bike rental shop. There is an automated bank machine here as well. The town also has two gas stations. We always try to stay in the tenting section at Lake Louise; the fact that an electrified fence surrounds it is of some comfort, given that it is right in the path of the wildlife.

Banff, Alberta

Banff is located just off the Trans Canada Highway, 34.2 miles (55 kilometers) east of Lake Louise and 80 miles (128 kilometers) west of Calgary. The Trans Canada Highway from Lake Louise to Calgary is a double lane and the distance covered between them is very quick, even in the heaviest of tourist traffic. Banff has three very large campgrounds as well as many hotels, cabins, cottages and bed & breakfasts. There are plenty of grocery stores, restaurants, laundry facilities, banks, bank machines, gas stations and many other amenities available here. Unbelievably, this town is actually within the park boundaries! When staying in Banff, we have usually stayed at

Tunnel Mountain III with fire pits. We did try out the one with electricity (Tunnel Mountain II), but found it to be a bit like staying in a parking lot. One of these times, we are going to stay at Two Jacks, which is considerably outside of town. Historically, the town of Banff has run transit out to the Tunnel Mountain campgrounds, but the last time we were there, it seems the service now only goes to the first campsite. Check with Parks Canada for more information on local transit in Banff.

Icefields Center/Wilcox Creek, Alberta

Located within the center of the IceFields Parkway, the Icefields Center is a tourist stop, information center and hotel. It is located 67 miles (108 kilometers) south of Jasper and 74 miles (119 kilometers) north of Lake Louise. There are no amenities outside of the center itself. You can rent a spot here in the parking lot to park your RV, however, this is a newer thing and I have always preferred to camp at Wilcox Creek, when we camp, we love our campfires and it gets pretty cold at night here.

Wilcox Creek Campground is located a few kilometers south of the Icefields Center. It is a wilderness campground that requires self registration (find a spot that has no tag on the post, park your RV in it and walk back and register). It has pit toilets, fire pits, potable drinking water, some cook shacks and no other amenities. You are truly camping in the wilderness here!

NOTE: there are no gas stations in the IceFields Center, the closest gas stations are Jasper 67 miles (108 kilometers) or Saskatchewan Crossing which is 31 miles (50 kilometers) to the south, insure that your fuel tank is full when leaving Jasper or Lake Louise. Also of note, you will find gas prices at Saskatchewan Crossing sometimes as much as 50% higher than elsewhere.

Now that I have mentioned the places where I think you should camp, we'll go on to talk about the actual things to see and do.

Darren Critchley

Section Two - What To Actually See And Do

Chapter Eight – Jasper and Area – 2 to 3 days

Jasper is located at the intersection of Highways 93 and 16. It is a fairly large town with almost all amenities you would need. It also has a fairly historic railway station where one can still catch a train on Canadian National's VIA rail. The Rocky Mountaineer also stops here. The railway station has been preserved as a historic site. If you are coming to the Rockies from either Northern Alberta (Edmonton) or the middle of British Columbia (Kamloops), then Jasper can be reached via Highway 16. If however, you are reaching the Rockies via Calgary or Revelstoke Highway 1 (Trans Canada Highway), then Jasper will need to be a side trip via Lake Louise on Highway 93.

There are several very large campsites in Jasper, Whistlers and Wapiti; both are run by Parks Canada. Wapiti is open throughout the year, and Whistlers is usually open from mid May to mid September. I prefer to stay in Whistlers, mainly because I can get a fire pit with electricity. Given that it has rained more times than I can count when I have been there, electricity comes in handy to keep the kids entertained with movies or what have you. There are many, many hotels, bed & breakfasts and cottages to rent in Jasper. If you are not staying in an RV, then I would suggest checking out the *TravelAlberta.com* website, it offers many deals for staying in hotels, B&B's and cottages in the Rockies. Even if you are in an RV, you might want to check that site out as well, often many of the attractions you are going to visit will have specials on that site.

Jasper is on the edge of the Rockies, which is why it sometimes attracts the wrong kind of weather. It has been a rare stay for us when it has been sunny here. If you were planning to visit Jasper via Lake Louise, then I would check with Parks Canada in Lake Louise to see what the weather is like in Jasper before leaving. It is a fairly short drive from there to Jasper, which means if there is a window of opportunity then take it. Even if it does rain, there are still plenty of things to do in Jasper that you will enjoy.

Jasper still maintains a lot of the Rocky Mountain charm that has disappeared in other towns in the Rockies. What I mean by this is that the tourist shops for the most part still cater to all types of tourists and you will actually find souvenirs that represent the town and the mountains. By comparison, Banff is now very focused on the Asian market and the souvenir shops reflect that, examples are stores that sell John Deer collectors items, rock and roll posters, and other western posters or paraphernalia. None of these items have anything to do with the Canadian Rockies. I must say though that Jasper is starting to go the same way, slowly the stores are changing. That being said, Jasper is still a very enjoyable walk, there are two main streets, both lined with shops and restaurants.

On the second street in, Patricia (from the main street through town – Connaught Drive), you will find a large launderette for doing laundry, which also has an Internet cafe. I have yet to find any free wifi spots in Jasper, but there is cell coverage in Jasper. Also on Patricia street you will find a grocery store, I recommend this one over the one on Connaught Drive, because the prices are more inline with a normal grocery store. The one on Connaught Drive seems to cater to the tourists and hence, groceries are priced accordingly.

We always thought there was little to Jasper other than the town and the tramway. It took a couple of rainy days of exploration to show us that there are other things to do and see in the area. We still continue to find new things in Jasper, which is very surprising, even as late as last year, we discovered another gem there which presented us with a new view of Jasper, that we had never seen before. To be honest, if it was not for another hobby of mine, Geocaching, I would not have found this place. Anyways, geocaching is a topic for another book of mine.

Jasper will require about two to three days to see everything in and around it, particularly if you exclude the Icefields Parkway. The major sites around Jasper include the tramway, Maligne Lake, Maligne Canyon, Mount Edith Cavell, and Athabasca Falls. These are the primary attractions that get all the attention, but there are more such as Pyramid Lake, Patricia Lake, Old Fort Point, Lac Beauvert, Annette & Edith Lakes and Medicine Lake. It is these gems that the rainy days helped us find. I'll talk about each one in more detail now.

Jasper Tramway – ½ day

Without a doubt, this is probably the best-known attraction around Jasper. The base is located 4.3 miles (7 kilometers) up the road from the Whistlers Campground on Whistlers Road. It is well posted and easy to find, in fact you can see it from pretty much anywhere in Jasper. The elevation is 4279 feet (1304 meters) at the base and a seven-minute trip up the tramway will bring you to an altitude of 7472 feet (2277 meters). At that point you can walk around the boardwalks, read the informative signs and take in the views! For the more adventurous you can then climb another 600 feet (183 meters) to the summit of the mountain where you will have a view unmatched by almost anything in the Rockies. You can see Mount Robson (the highest mountain in the Canadian Rockies) to the east all covered in snow. You can see the town of Jasper and look down the valley to the south, which follows the continental divide.

Taking in this attraction requires a good clear day, so it is very weather dependent, in fact, it took our family at least five trips to finally get on this attraction! It is definitely worthwhile to go on this one. I've only had the opportunity to go up it once, but will do so again when time and weather permit. I would rate this as one of the top ten best things to see or do in the Canadian Rockies.

Check the Jasper Tramway website for up to date details: *http://www.jaspertramway.com/*
Here's a tip, the tramway and Maligne Lake boat tour are often combined into one package. Check the Jasper Tramway website, the *TravelAlberta.com* website, or the brochures handed out in most souvenir shops in town for the discount package.

Jasper Tramway will take up approximately a half day; depending upon how much time you spend on the top. The ride up and down will take approximately 15 minutes plus wait time. The parking lot is within ten minutes of town, or literally minutes from the Whistlers Campground.

Maligne Lake – 1 Day With Maligne Canyon Included

Maligne Lake is located 27 miles (44 Kilometers) out of Jasper on Maligne Road, the same road used to visit Maligne Canyon and Medicine Lake. The lake itself is 14 miles (22.5 kilometers) long. It is one of the most fantastic drives through the Rockies, and that alone is worth the drive. Along the drive you will come across Medicine Lake, a pretty but mysterious lake that we will talk about later.

When you arrive at Maligne Lake, there is plenty of parking, for cars and RV's. There is a restaurant and washroom facilities. There is a very famous boat tour here, as well as canoe rentals, guided fishing, whitewater rafting and hiking.

The main feature here is the scenic boat cruise and I would recommend this to anyone! This is one of only two lakes in the Canadian Rockies that has motorized boats on it and thus, one of two lakes where you can actually take a boat tour. The boat tour takes about 90 minutes for a round trip and takes you to the famous Spirit Island. Spirit Island is featured on many post cards of the Canadian Rockies as well as posters, books and other souvenirs. Spirit Island is the most famous landmark of the Canadian Rockies, mainly due to a picture of it being posted in Grand Central Station in New York, but the tour guide will tell you more about this.

The boat tour takes you 8.7 miles (14 kilometers) up Maligne Lake, a very long and narrow lake that is a beautiful color of turquoise typical of most Rocky Mountain Lakes. Spirit Island is the furthest that the tour boat can go, after that, the lake is deemed a protected wilderness area accessible only by non-motorized craft. The lake itself actually contains fish, although the trout were not native to this lake, someone early on stocked the lake to attract tourists and the fish took.

If you plan on taking this boat tour, then the best thing to do is try to check the weather in the Maligne Lake office in downtown Jasper. It takes a bit of convincing, but you can ask them to call up to the lake and let you know what the weather is like. At that point, if the weather is good, it will take you an hour to drive to Maligne Lake – it is up to you to choose whether or not to purchase tickets in town and then drive up. The boat tour is very popular and you are taking a chance in not purchasing tickets ahead of time. That is unless you have time to wait for the next tour when you arrive. The tours run from 10am until 5 pm on the hour in the summer. Check the Maligne Lake website for up to date information (*http://www.malignelake.com*) as well as available tours and shuttle buses.

The boat tour itself is fantastic! The color of the water is unbelievable and you are surrounded on all sides by beautiful mountains. There are several glaciers you can see as well. The boats are large, with large windows to see out of, as well, you can take turns with the other passengers to go out on the rear deck and take photographs. For the uniqueness of this boat tour, I would rate this as one of the top ten best things to see or do in the Canadian Rockies.

Maligne Canyon – up to 2 hours

Maligne Canyon is located just outside Jasper 7.2 miles (11.5

kilometers) on Maligne Road. It is open year round and is a self-guided tour that follows the canyon and you cross six bridges on the tour. There is a restaurant and gift shop located near the start of the canyon, furthest away from Jasper. There are several parking lots along the route that you can stop at and view different parts of the canyon, or you can elect to walk the entire length, which takes about one hour one way.

The most popular tour is to park near the top, where the gift shop & restaurant are located and visit the 1st and 2nd bridge, that tour takes about 15 minutes for the round trip. We had visited the canyon several times, but had missed the fossils in the bedrock next to the canyon! Thanks to Parks Canada's Junior Explorer program that started in 2011 and my then nine year old daughter, we spent the better part of an hour near the 1st bridge crawling around on our hands and knees (with grandpa) trying to find and identify six different fossils found in the rocks there. PS, if it is still running and you have kids, each National Park has a program called Junior Explorers, which will give your kids a few more activities to do in the Parks, while learning something.

Maligne Canyon is an excellent thing to do if it is raining! Because you are in a canyon, there is very little in the way of scenery (other than the canyon) to see. The canyon can be enjoyed in the rain, although if you are looking for fossils, it may not be as enjoyable crawling around on hands and knees. In fact, as long as you keep your camera dry, you are most likely to take better pictures under an overcast sky.

I mentioned that Maligne Canyon was open year round. In winter there are guided Ice Walks through the Canyon! This is something that I have not had the opportunity to do yet, but it is definitely on my to do list. In fact, I expect that the experience will probably make my top ten list of things to see and do in the Canadian Rockies.

Medicine Lake

I mentioned this lake in the Maligne Lake section. It is a lake that you pass on your way to Maligne Lake, about halfway to Maligne Lake 16.8 miles (27 kilometers). I had mentioned it is a little bit mysterious, well that is because, depending upon when you visit it, it may not be there! In fact, it is not actually a lake, but an area where the Maligne River backs up and fills out the area. The lake actually drains through an underground system – another mysterious part of the lake. It took scientists a while (and some dye) to figure out just where the water went. The biodegradable dye that was introduced to Medicine Lake showed up in many of the lakes and rivers in the area, leading scientists to believe the underground channels are one of most extensive underground cave systems in the Western Hemisphere. Because the drain is so small, the water backs up and forms a lake. This lake disappears as water levels get lower in late fall and winter. Once the spring snow starts to melt, the lake returns. It is a pretty lake to stop at and take pictures. There is a picnic area where you can stop, take pictures and read the information signs.

Visiting Maligne Lake, Medicine Lake and Maligne Canyon will take up the better part of a day. The drive from Jasper to Maligne Lake is 1 hour each way. The boat tour if you take it is 90 minutes. Add to that a possible snack at the restaurant and taking pictures and you've probably used up half a day. If you add to that stopping to take photographs of Medicine Lake and then hike parts or all of the Maligne Canyon, you will have used up the better part of a day. You could finish this off by visiting Beauvert Lake and Old Fort Point as they are close to the end of Maligne Canyon; I will talk more about these later in the chapter.

Mount Edith Cavell – ½ day

Mount Edith Cavell is located about 18 miles (29 kilometers) south of Jasper on the Cavell Road, which is accessible from Highway 93. This road has a lot of twists, turns and switchbacks. It is often a little bumpy too, due to frost heaves. Travel trailers are not allowed on this road and there is a pull off at the start of it to drop your travel trailer. Also vehicles longer than 19 feet (6 meters) are not recommended to use the road due to the tight corners. Parks Canada notes that vehicles 22 feet (7 meters) and longer cannot navigate the corners and are banned from the road.

Mount Edith Cavell is open from June to October, has a decent sized parking lot at the end of it and is a lovely walk for all ages. There are some picnic tables and pit toilets. There is a loop trail (Path of the Glacier Trail) that follows the path of a receded glacier around the edge of the valley and then down into it, returning via the valley bottom. At the end of the trail is what you are looking for, the Angel Hanging Glacier, which sits on the side of Mount Edith Cavell. At the base of the glacier is a moraine with lots of little icebergs floating in it, even in the middle of summer, if you are lucky, you can grab a piece, but it is very cold in the water!

There is another hike here called The Cavell Meadows trail, it climbs considerably and goes to a meadow where flowers may be in bloom. I say may be in bloom because at the sub alpine level, flowers bloom for a very short period. Your best bet is to check with Parks Canada in Jasper to find out if the flowers are in bloom (and to check out any recent bear sightings in the area). Just a quick note, always check with Parks Canada before heading off into any mountain trails, some trails are closed at certain times due to wildlife mating seasons, or require a group of people to enter.

I recommend taking this tour only in fairly decent weather. If it is raining hard, in all likelihood, the Angel Glacier will be obstructed by cloud and you will see nothing.

Mount Edith Cavell will take up about a half day to drive up, do the Path of the Glacier Trail, enjoy yourself and drive back. There is one picture opportunity on the road up, where you can pull over and take some pictures of the landscape. It is a large pull off on the right hand side of the road.

Patricia and Pyramid Lakes – 2 hours

There are some gems hidden above Jasper that we didn't find until we were stuck in the rain and decided that we needed to dig a little deeper in Jasper to see what was there. We had seen these lakes mentioned on the tourist guide and decided to take a look. It is approximately 4.3 miles (7 kilometers) to the lakes and both have ample parking, although if Pyramid is busy, you may have to park further down the road. Access to both lakes is via Pyramid Lake Road, which is pretty much the furthest road from the main road (Connaught Drive). It is well posted on many of Jasper's streets and is easy to find.

Patricia Lake is a small lake just outside of Jasper and really is just another lake; its only real significance is that during World War II, a secret project called Project Habbakuk took place here. They planned to build an unsinkable aircraft carrier from an ice-based material called Pykrete. There is a pull off here and information boards telling more about the story. Also in this area are several trails if you like gentle hikes.

Pyramid Lake is a real gem, located just outside Jasper on Pyramid Lake Road. As you come to Pyramid Lake, you will see a dock with some paddle boats and other boats tied up. On your right hand side you will see a resort and an ice cream shop. This is a nice place to stop, have an ice cream, maybe take a swim or stroll, but keep going for now! The real gem is further down the road. You will come to a parking lot on the left hand side of the road, if it is full, go a little further and there is a cul de sac where the road ends, you can park here and walk back. From the parking lot is a beautiful stroll across a bridge onto an island. You can walk around this island and have some fantastic views of different mountains around Jasper. Mount Edith Cavell being one of them and of course Pyramid Mountain being another. There are signs around the walk that tell you about your surroundings and also point out the various mountains. If you stop in the middle of the bridge, you can see fish swimming below. All in all, this is a beautiful, peaceful ½ hour stroll around the island. As always, it is better in sunny weather, but we've done it in the rain too, you just don't see as many mountains.

Once your done with your walk, you can now go back to the resort and enjoy some of that ice cream.

Old Fort Point and Lac Beauvert – 3 hours

Old Fort Point

Old Fort Point is a short steep hike that will give you a view of Jasper and the surrounding Rocky Mountains. It is located about 1 mile (1.6 kilometers) out of Jasper. You follow Highway 93A either from downtown Jasper or off of Highway 93. Then follow the signs to Old Fort Point. As with most points of interest in the National Parks, it is well marked with signs. After crossing the Miette River, you will come to a parking lot on your right. In the parking lot you will find an information board showing the trail information and the trailhead.

We only discovered this gem last year because we were looking for a geocache. For those interested, a geocache is a hidden treasure that people hide throughout the world and you search for these treasures using a GPS to find them. It is a fun family sport, which I will be covering in a future book, but more information can be found by checking out *http://www.geocaching.com/*

We had driven past this place many times when heading over to Lac Beauvert (which we'll talk about in a minute) and ignored it as just another hike into the wilderness. Well, were we ever wrong, this is a steep but fantastic hike on the open hillside giving you fantastic views

31

of Jasper. The full hike is about 2.2 miles (3.5 kilometers) round trip and is a constant climb on the way up, the last little bit being extremely steep and rocky. Of course, the first bit up all the steps is a challenge too, and very impressive to see how they built all those steps.

After seeing this last year, this is a must do in Jasper, even in bad weather you will still get a view of the town, but in clear weather, the view is much more rewarding. From the top of the hill you can see Lac Beauvert and the Jasper Park Lodge, as well as Annette & Edith Lakes. You will also see the Miette and Athabasca Rivers where they meet.

Lac Beauvert

Lac Beauvert is just down the road from the Old Fort Point and is where the road ends. There is a parking lot and you can get out and look at the lake. There are picnic tables and it's a nice spot to have a picnic. It's a beautiful little lake surrounded by mountains and the photographic opportunities abound. Across the Lake is the Jasper Park Lodge. The water is a deep green color and not the typical turquoise color of Rocky Mountain Lakes.

Annette & Edith Lakes – 1 hour

Annette & Edit Lakes are just outside Jasper on Highway 16 and are accessed by turning on to Maligne Road but staying to the right after crossing the Athabasca River. It is a short distance to each lake and they are just some pretty lakes to look at. In an evening or early morning, they are usually calm and one can capture some beautiful reflections of the Rocky Mountains in them.

There are picnic tables at both of them and one can enjoy a quiet picnic at either one – they are rarely busy.

Athabasca Falls – 1 hour

This can be included in Jasper as it is so close to Jasper, but I am going to put it in the Icefields Parkway chapter, right after this one. So see you in the next chapter. . .

Darren Critchley

Chapter Nine – The Icefields Parkway – 1 to 3 Days

The Icefields Parkway is undoubtedly one of the most spectacular roadways in the world. For about 146 miles (235 kilometers) you follow the continental divide in a wide valley surrounded on both sides by magnificent jagged peaks. Driving this road is definitely in my top ten things to see and do in the Canadian Rockies. You will see glaciers, turquoise lakes, snowfields and mountains. There are many stops along this road to view the sites. While it only takes about three hours to drive this road straight through, if you stop at a lot of the sites, it can take two or three days. I am going to write this as if we are coming from Jasper to Lake Louise and tell you about how much time each site will take. We usually camp at Wilcox Creek for about two nights if we are doing a lot of activities in the area. You can also stay at the Icefields Center in the hotel or parking lot if you have an RV. There is also another hotel located at Saskatchewan Crossing. My favorite is Wilcox Creek; it is a wilderness campsite with lots of spots, a sani dump and fresh water.

There are many stops throughout this highway to stop and take pictures of the breathtaking scenery. Realizing that tourists will want to stop to admire, Parks Canada has made sure there are lots of posted pull offs to safely allow tourists to enjoy.

This highway is a purely recreational highway, having no other reason to exist, than to allow tourists to see some of the most fantastic scenery the Canadian Rockies has to offer. There are no fuel stations in the Icefields Parkway, with the exception of Saskatchewan Crossing, where you can often find fuel as much as 50% higher than Jasper and Lake Louise. So plan ahead when you are going down this road, make sure the gas tank is full.

Athabasca Falls – 1 hour

Athabasca Falls is located 18.6 miles (30 kilometers) south of Jasper on Highway 93, the Icefields Parkway. It is approximately 30 minutes driving time. There is lots of parking here for RV's, buses and cars. There are pit toilets and picnic tables at this site. It takes roughly ½ hour to drive to here from Jasper.

These falls are not very high, only 75 feet (23 meters) high, but they are fairly wide and a lot of water is flowing, well the entire Athabasca River is going over these falls. Over the centuries, these falls have created a short canyon and some potholes. There is a bridge and walkways all around the falls allowing you to view the falls, potholes and canyon. Of course there are interpretive signs all around telling you about the details of the falls as well as the geological happenings to make the canyons and potholes. One of the canyons has been abandoned by the river and you can walk down it to a look out point over the Athabasca River and can climb down to the river itself.

The Athabasca Falls are a great stop on the Icefields parkway and worth the hour it will take to walk around them. This is an easy stop with good parking and no climbing or clambering. In fact, there are signs everywhere telling you to remain on the trails/walkways, because the rocks around the falls are very wet and slippery.

Sunwapta Falls – 1 hour

This is another stop along the Icefields Parkway, located about 34 miles (55 kilometers) south of Jasper, approximately 40 minutes driving time. 10 minutes driving time from Athabasca Falls or 35 minutes from the Icefields Center. The parking lot is a short drive off of the main highway. As always, the site is well posted, but there is only one sign and then the turn off. It seems that warning signs in the National Parks are a rarity rather than the norm.

There is a lodge here with rooms, a restaurant, washrooms and a gift shop. It is a bit of a walk to the actual falls, but well worthwhile. These falls are a bit higher than the Athabasca falls. They have a drop of 60 feet (18.5 meters) with a width of 30 feet (9.1 meters).

There are two sets of falls here, an upper and lower. Most people only visit the upper as they are close by and require very little effort to see. The source of these falls is the Athabasca Glacier and these falls have the most volume in late spring and early summer.

Icefields Center/Athabasca Glacier – ½ day or more

This is the centerpiece of the Icefields Parkway, the Athabasca Glacier. It is located 64 miles (103 kilometers) from Jasper about 75 minutes driving time and 82 miles (132 kilometers) from Lake Louise about 90 minutes driving time. This is one of the largest icefields in Canada and feeds three different oceans from this one ice sheet. There is a hotel with a large parking lot here that is the Icefields Center. It is a popular tourist stop and has a bit of a museum downstairs. You can walk around the Icefields Center to look at the information signs, visit the souvenir shop or book a ride on a Snow Coach that will take you out onto the Athabasca Glacier.

If you're planning on staying over night, then I would recommend either booking a spot at the Icefields center – they have spots set aside in the parking lot for RV's, or drive a few kilometers south to Wilcox Creek Campground, a wilderness campground. Once you have a spot booked at either place, then you can go out and enjoy the sites in the Icefields.

Athabasca Glacier – 1 to 2 hours

From the parking lot across from the Icefields Center, you can park and then hike all the way up to the foot of the glacier. There are signs along the way marking where the glacier toe once touched. It starts at something like 1910 at the highway and the markers progress up the hill until you reach the ice. Note: it is a steep uphill climb.

Depending upon conditions, you may even be able to go out onto the ice field itself. Parks Canada usually has a section roped off so you can walk out onto it. Extreme caution is required and you need to keep a hold of your children, people have fallen into crevasses before and died from exposure. If you are not able to walk out onto the ice, then you still have two further options to get on the ice. The first is a guided tour that can be booked from the Icefields Center or taking a ride on a Snow Coach, those big six wheeled buses.

Icefields Center – 1 hour

The Icefields Center is a hotel, restaurant, office, museum, gift shop and tourist information booth all in one building. Downstairs there is a bit of a museum with local history and exhibits that teach you about the Athabasca Glacier. There is a nice souvenir shop, a restaurant and washrooms. It is a busy, busy place. It has some nice steps and patios around it, where one can take in the views of the Athabasca Glacier, while learning more about it. This is also the place to book a Snow Coach tour. Note the Icefields Center is open from mid April to mid October.

Snow Coach – 80 minutes

The Snow Coach is a six wheeled all wheel drive bus that takes you out onto the Athabasca Glacier. You purchase your ticket at the Icefields Center and then board a regular bus that drives you up to the side of the Athabasca Glacier, while telling you about the history and geology of the area. Once you get to the loading area for the Snow Coaches, you are instructed in which area to wait and when ready, you are asked to climb up into the Snow Coach. Inside the Snow Coach looks pretty much like any other bus, except it stands about 10 feet above the pavement.

The Snow Coach leaves the parking lot and drives down a very steep embankment onto the ice. There is a large puddle at the bottom that they drive through, which allows them to clean the debris off of the tires so it isn't tracked all over the icefield.

The Snow Coach drives out to the middle of the glacier and then stops and lets you out so you can walk around. A "liftee" at the Sulphur Mountain Gondola gave us a couple of good tips about visiting the icefield and I will share them with you. Number one take a warm jacket with you, it is COLD on the ice, even in the middle of August on the hottest day. There is a wind that comes down that ice that will chill you in minutes. The second tip was to take an empty water bottle with you so you can scoop up some of the ice-cold water that has melted from the glacier. It is said that this water is 700 years old and is supposed to have qualities similar to the fountain of youth!

After visiting the Columbia Icefields for many, many years, we finally took the Snow Coach ride last year and were very glad we did it. Nowhere else on earth can you get into a six wheeled bus with ten foot tires and drive out onto a sheet of ice that is as deep as the CN Tower in Ontario is high. For that reason, I would rate this as one of the top ten best things to see or do in the Canadian Rockies.

For more up to date information on the Snow Coach, please check their website at *http://www.explorerockies.com/columbia-icefield/*

Wilcox Pass Hike – ½ day to 1 day

At Wilcox Creek campground there is the trailhead for Wilcox Pass. This is a 6.8 mile (11 kilometer) hike (one way) that goes around Wilcox Mountain and reappears back on the Icefields Parkway via Tangle Creek. Now you are probably wondering why there is a hike that goes off the highway and into the mountains and then comes back out on the highway 4.3 miles (7 kilometers) later. Well, you see, when this area was first explored, the Athabasca Glacier was all the way across the valley. In fact, where the Icefields Center now stands, was completely under the glacier back in 1895 when Walter Wilcox made the first recorded trip into the area by a white man.

You do not have to do the entire trail to enjoy this hike; in fact, you only need to go about a ½ mile (1 kilometer or so) up the trail to take in some extraordinary views of the Athabasca Glacier and the Saskatchewan Glacier. If you do go up to the summit of the pass (1.2 miles or 2km from the trail head), you will also be rewarded with even better views of the surrounding glaciers. On top of that, you will have hiked above the treeline of the Canadian Rockies, a feat that not many can brag about, and the nice thing is, it is very easy to do that here. If you do choose to go all the way to the summit of Wilcox Pass, you will have gained 1,099 feet (335 meters) in altitude from the trailhead and will have hiked above the treeline in one of North America's most beautiful places. To achieve the same height on a hike elsewhere in the Rockies would require some strenuous hiking.

If you plan on doing the whole thing, perhaps you can meet up with another group and arrange for one vehicle to be at the parking lot at the other end of the trail, that way you only need do the pass once. Without a vehicle waiting for you at the other end, it can be a very, very long day. Once in the pass, things level off and it is easy for much of the way, but eventually you need to drop back down to the road.

Saskatchewan Crossing – ½ hour to 1 hour

Saskatchewan Crossing is a motel, restaurant, pub, souvenir shop and gas station where Highway 93 meets Highway 11 (David Thompson Highway), which goes to Red Deer. This is the only gas station on the Icefields Parkway and is located 48 miles (77 kilometers) from Lake Louise, about 55 minutes driving time.

It is named Saskatchewan Crossing because the early fur traders that came through here made the crossing of the Saskatchewan River just down the road from it. Also, three rivers converge here, the Mistaya River, the Howse River and the North Saskatchewan River.

This is a nice place to stop and take some pictures; beautiful mountains on all sides surround the resort. You can also take in a snack, beverage or souvenir while here too.

Mistaya Canyon – ½ hour to 1 hour

The Mistaya Canyon is noted by a large sign and a pull off on the side of the road 45 miles (72 kilometers) from Lake Louise, about 50 minutes drive. This is a relatively short hike down into the valley. You eventually come to a bridge that crosses the canyon. You can then see the canyon carved into the bedrock. Potholes and a natural arch in the canyon walls are also geological features that you will see. The trail is 1/3 of a mile (0.5 kilometers) from the highway down to the valley below, about 10 minutes one way. This was another of those gems that we always drove by. We finally stopped in 2011 after our excursion on the Snow Coaches. Yet again, another stop worthy of your time, the canyon walls and the water rushing through them are spectacular.

Bow Summit and Peyto Lake – 1 to 2 hours

Located about 25 miles (40 kilometers) from Lake Louise, about 30 minutes drive, is the Bow Summit and Peyto Lake, (pronounced pea-toe). There is a parking lot here with lots of room for RV's & cars, as well as an upper parking lot for handicapped and bus passengers. The walk to Peyto Lake is about ½ mile (1 kilometer) from the parking lot and is mostly up hill.

You will come to an observation platform that over looks Peyto Lake and the Icefields Parkway. You have a great view of the lake here and it's a photographers dream! Peyto Lake is said to be one of the most turquoise colored lakes in all of the Canadian Rockies. If you have seen any brochures or posters of the Canadian Rockies, you have most likely seen this lake; it resembles the head of a dog or wolf.

If you visit in July or August, you should be able to see the wildflowers in bloom. There are many interpretative signs along the trail to educate you on the flowers and the wildlife. The trail itself is actually paved, so most people should be able to access the trail. Those who cannot or are in a wheelchair can be dropped off at the upper parking lot.

The observation deck is usually busy throughout the summer, and very difficult to get a picture of the lake without a bunch of tourists in the picture. Here's a tip on getting a better picture, the trail continues on further from the observation deck and comes to a large clearing. From here you can take a picture of the lake, uninterrupted by tourists or trees.

This is an easy and short hike to see one of the most beautiful lakes in the Canadian Rockies. Again for me, this was a lake that we passed for many years and never stopped until a friend once asked me if I had ever been there. It took me two more years since I was told of this lake before we finally stopped here, but I have been returning ever since.

Crowfoot Glacier/Bow Glacier & Bow Lake – ½ hour to 1 hour

About 21 miles (34 kilometers) from Lake Louise, about 25 minutes driving time, is Bow Lake. A brilliantly colored glacier fed lake that rivals the waters of the Caribbean for color. Above it stand two glaciers easily seen from either of the two pull offs, the Crowfoot Glacier and the Bow Glacier. There is a pull off closest to Lake Louise that offers the best view of the Crowfoot Glacier. Then further down the road, there is an actual turn off to go to a resort. Here there is a large parking lot and washrooms. You can then walk down to the Bow Lake and take a picture of the Bow Glacier above the lake.

The resort has washrooms, rooms, a souvenir shop and a small restaurant. This is a busy place in summer as many buses stop here and let their passengers out.

Unfortunately, you will not catch the color of the lake from either of these spots. If you want to catch the color of the lake in all its glory, then you need to go north along the highway towards Jasper. As you climb away from the lake, look back. Eventually you will reach enough altitude to be above the lake, with the afternoon sun shining on it, it goes a color of blue that is unrivaled anywhere. The best two times to photograph this lake are early morning, the lake is calm and you can take some fantastic reflection shots. The other time is late afternoon with the sun shining on the lake from above the lake.

Herbert Lake – ¼ hour

Herbert Lake is a small lake about 5 minutes out of Lake Louise on Highway 93. It looks like it used to be a campsite, but is now a picnic area. If you visit this lake early in the morning or early evening, you can take some fantastic reflection shots of the surrounding mountains. Other than a quick picnic, there is nothing much more to say about this lake.

Because of the unmatched beauty of this drive, I would rate the Icefields Parkway as one of the top ten best things to see or do in the Canadian Rockies.

Darren Critchley

Chapter Ten – Lake Louise – 2 to 3 days

Lake Louise is located on Highway 1, the Trans Canada Highway between the towns of Field, British Columbia and Banff, Alberta. It is a small village that exists mainly for tourists and it is the highest community in Canada. It has two gas stations, several restaurants, many hotels, cabins, B&B's, cottages and one very large campground run by Parks Canada. There is a small strip mall here that has a small grocery store, candy shop, liquor store, bakery, small post office and several souvenir shops. There is also a bank machine located at the strip mall. Unfortunately there are no laundry facilities in Lake Louise and as of this writing; I have not been able to find any free Wifi, even though several websites say otherwise.

Lake Louise started life as a stop on the Canadian Pacific Railway, at the station of Laggan, later renamed Lake Louise. There is still a railway station at Lake Louise, which is now a restaurant. This is not the original railway station that was built in the 1800's, that railway station now sits at the Calgary Heritage Park.
The sole purpose of the railway station here was so that guests could go up to the Chateau at Lake Louise. At one time, there used to be a tramway to run passengers from the railway station, to the Chateau. The tramway has long since disappeared, but you can still walk the trail to the Chateau from the village.

Lake Louise is a beautiful lake with turquoise colored water. Peaks on all sides surround it and the backdrop is Victoria Glacier. You really cannot get much more picturesque than this! There is a lot to do and see around Lake Louise, particularly if you are a hiker. The CPR brought in many guides to help its guests hike up the surrounding mountains, so there are lots of well-marked trails in the area.

The major attractions around Lake Louise would be the actual lake, Chateau Lake Louise, the hikes, canoeing, horseback riding, taking a gondola ride to the top of the Lake Louise ski resort, Bow Summit, Peyto Lake, the Natural Bridge at Field, Takakkaw Falls, Emerald Lake, the Burgess Shale, Lake O'Hara and Moraine Lake.

Truthfully, you could spend an entire week here and still not see it all.

Crowfoot Glacier/Bow Glacier & Bow Lake, Bow Summit and Peyto Lake

I have already covered these places in the previous chapter, but they are so close to Lake Louise, that they should be mentioned here. They are found along Highway 93.

Bow Lake, the Crowfoot Glacier and the Bow Glacier are About 21 miles (34 kilometers) from Lake Louise, about 25 minutes driving time. Bow Summit and Peyto Lake are located about 25 miles (40 kilometers) from Lake Louise, about 30 minutes drive.

Please go to the previous chapter for more details and information on these sites.

Lake Louise and Chateau Lake Louise ½ day to 1 day

You could easily spend an entire day at Lake Louise and the Chateau. There are lots of easy walking trails around the lake, which allow you great views of the Chateau. There are also plenty of flower gardens and landscaping around the Chateau to look at. The Chateau at the time of this writing is run by Fairmont Hotels. The Chateau contains two pubs, several restaurants, an ice cream shop and many souvenir shops. There is a bank machine located within the hotel. There are washrooms available here for public use and most of the main floor of the hotel is open to the public to walk around. It is worth a walk around this hotel, to see the architecture of a grand old hotel. The original hotel was built by the Canadian Pacific Railway in the late 1800's and rebuilt entirely several times due to fires. The CPR Hotels in the Canadian Rockies were often referred to as castles in the mountains.

To get to Lake Louise, follow the road from the village, it is well marked. Lake Louise is one of the busiest places in the Rockies, and your best bet for getting a parking spot is early morning or early evening.

Lake Louise itself has a trail going around the front of the lake and on one side of it. The other side is inaccessible due to the steep cliffs of Fairview Mountain next to it. The front of the lake, closest to the hotel has been decorated with stonework and steps that go into the lake. However, the lake is extremely cold, even in summer the water is lucky to reach 50° F (10° C), the lake is fed by glaciers and you can see them at the end of the lake as a magnificent backdrop. In fact, it is because of being fed by glaciers, that gives the lake its turquoise color. The rocks that the glaciers cross are ground down into fine dust called rock flour. This rock flour then becomes suspended in the water. The rock flour only allows the blue spectrum of light to refract from it, therefore, you end up with the turquoise color. In all my visits to Lake Louise, I have ever only seen two people swimming in it. I see lots of people dipping their feet into it, but the cold makes them pull it out right away.

You can take a leisurely walk to the other end of the lake 1.18 miles (1.9 kilometers) one-way. The path is flat and paved, making it an easy walk for anyone. If you wish to continue beyond the end of the lake, you can hike to the Plain of the Six Glaciers Teahouse, 2.24 miles (3.6 kilometers) and then on to the Plain of the Six Glaciers, a further 0.8 of a mile (1.3 kilometers). This hike is a fairly easy one, as most of the way you are pretty level, with not much climbing. There are plenty more trails around that do involve climbing and we will mention those soon enough.

Back at the lake, you can rent a canoe and paddle around the lake. Or if you prefer, you can rent a horse and take a guided tour around the lake, to the Plain of the Six Glaciers or to the Teahouse at Lake Agnes.

Given the picturesque setting of Lake Louise, its history, hikes and teahouses, I would rate this as one of the top ten best things to see or do in the Canadian Rockies.

The Teahouse, Lake Agnes and The Big Beehive – ½ day

Perched above Lake Louise, is a wonderful gem called Lake Agnes and it has a teahouse on the edge of it. All of the wood and other supplies for building the teahouse were carried up by people, as there is no road to it. Even today, employees hike all of the food & beverages, as well as the garbage in and out of the teahouse.

To get to the teahouse, you follow the Lake Agnes Trail, which is well marked from the hotel grounds. The distance is about 1.9 miles (3.1 kilometers) from the Chateau and this is a fairly steep climb as you will be gaining about 1325 feet (403 meters) in altitude. This is a hike that is well worth it! The last few feet before the teahouse, you come out of the forest to a waterfall on the side of a rock face, and to the right of and above that waterfall is the teahouse, perched on the edge of a cliff. Well it isn't really on the edge of a cliff, but it sure looks like it. From the waterfall, you then climb a rather lengthy set of stairs to bring you to the teahouse. The view at this point is beyond words, you are looking at a lake of a deep blue color surrounded on all sides by jagged peaks. There is a creek that comes out of the lake, runs past the teahouse and becomes the waterfall. It is like something right out of a fable.

Now that you are here, you can go in the teahouse and enjoy a beverage or snack. Read some of the information signs or just take in the view. For those that want to go further, you can. It is about 0.8 of a mile (1.3 kilometers) around Lake Agnes, where you can then ascend a series of switchbacks to climb 443 feet (135 meters) up to the Big Beehive.

The Big Beehive is a roundish shaped piece of rock that you may have noticed on your hike up to Lake Agnes, its pretty hard to miss and it looks like a beehive. At the top of it, there is a fire watch station, where you can look out over Lake Louise and the Chateau. You've climbed to an altitude of 7448 feet (2270 meters) to get to this view and it has been worth every bit of effort to climb the 1768 feet (539 meters) from the Chateau below.

For the storybook like setting of Lake Agnes and the Teahouse, I would rate this as one of the top ten best things to see or do in the Canadian Rockies.

There are many other trails around Lake Louise that climb up to the various mountains in the area. As there are far too many to mention in this book, I will mention one more that stands out, Fairview Mountain. The rest you can stop in at the Parks Canada center in Lake Louise and obtain trail guides and information. One could literally spend days hiking all the trails around Lake Louise.

Fairview Mountain – 1 day

Fairview Mountain is a 9002 foot (2744 meter) pyramid shaped mountain to the left of Lake Louise. You can't miss Fairview; it towers above everything in your view from the Chateau. Guess what, there is a nice trail that goes to the top of it! This is actually a very strenuous hike, but if you are up to it, it will reward you with astounding views of the lakes below, and the entire valley. The hike will take you 3322 feet (1012 meters) above the Chateau and you will do it in 2.9 miles (4.7 kilometers). Depending upon your speed, this climb will take about six or seven hours for a round trip. The first 2.1 miles (3.4 kilometers) is gradual up hill hiking to bring you to a valley next to Saddleback Mountain at an altitude of 7644 feet (2330 meters). Here you can rest, have lunch or a snack, before hiking up the last 1358 feet (414 meters) of Fairview Mountain in 0.8 of a mile (1.3 kilometers). The last section is the hardest; it is very steep with loose rocks and gravel. It takes a lot of effort to get up the final part of the mountain. Finally you will reach the top of Fairview Mountain and will have a full 360 degree view of the valley and lakes surrounding you. There is a plaque on the top of the mountain, and the very tip is about 10 feet (3 meters) wide and about 50 feet (15 meters) long. With the Victoria Glacier behind you, the pictures taken up here are just astounding. For the fantastic 360 degree view of a very beautiful place, I would rate this as one of the top ten best things to see or do in the Canadian Rockies.

Lake Louise Gondola – ½ day

Across Highway 1, the Trans Canada Highway, from the village, there is a ski hill, with lifts and gondolas. Throughout the summer, you can take a gondola up to the top of the ski hill, walk around and enjoy the view. You can hike further up the mountain as well, although there is little need as the view here is fantastic. If you choose, you can take in a buffet on top of the mountain in the Lodge of the Ten Peaks. You will also find an interpretative center at the top of the gondola, where you can learn more about the locals that live on the mountain. By locals we of course mean the wildlife. One can also take a 45 minute guided tour at the top of the mountain, to learn more about the area, and the wildlife.

Coming down the mountain, you have your choice of gondola or open chair lift. We chose the open chair lift so as to take pictures. Watch the ground closely as you go up or down the mountain; you have a pretty good chance to spot a grizzly bear or other wildlife. The website for the Lake Louise Gondola even states that it is one of the best places for Grizzly Bear viewing in the Canadian Rockies.
For up to date information on prices and hours of operation, please check the Lake Louise Gondola website at

http://www.skilouise.com/

The view from the top of the mountain overlooks the valley and Lake Louise; you can really capture the color of Lake Louise from here. For the fantastic view, I would rate this as one of the top ten best things to see or do in the Canadian Rockies.

Moraine Lake – ½ day

Moraine Lake is located 9.3 miles (15 kilometers) from Lake Louise Village, about 20 minutes; this is one lake you will want to see. It is in a valley called the Valley of the Ten Peaks and the lake itself, with some of the ten peaks, used to be on the Canadian $20 bill. You may have already seen this lake on a postcard or in some sort of advertising for the Canadian Rockies; it is a very beautiful lake. It has a very vivid blue color to it, particularly in the afternoon.

Moraine Lake is one of the busiest lakes for tourists in the Canadian Rockies. Like Lake Louise, expect a lot of people, particularly in the summer months. The best time to see Moraine Lake is early morning or early evening if you wish to avoid the crowds. However, if you want to see it in all its glory, then mid afternoon is the best time to go there. You will have a tough time finding parking, but if you do, you will be rewarded with a beautiful vibrant blue color on the lake.

There is a large pile of rocks, which scientists cannot agree on where they came from, that you can climb to the top of and get a great view of the lake. For the vibrant color, and the ten peaks behind it, I would rate this as one of the top ten best things to see or do in the Canadian Rockies.

Natural Bridge and Emerald Lake – ½ day

Located 18.6 miles (30 kilometers) west of Lake Louise, about a ½ hours driving time, is the Natural Bridge and Emerald Lake. These sites are located in Yoho National Park in British Columbia.

The Natural Bridge

The Natural Bridge is a natural rock bridge that has formed across the Kicking Horse River. At one time it was a waterfall, and over the eons, the water bored through the rock and formed a bridge. There is a large parking lot here and this site is not that busy. It is easily accessible and there is no climbing or hiking involved.

Emerald Lake

Emerald Lake is an aptly named lake that is located about 15 minutes further down the road from the Natural Bridge. There is a souvenir shop here and a resort. There are public washrooms and a picnic area. A trail follows the lake and is 3.23 miles (5.2 kilometers) long and takes approximately 2.5 hours to complete. There is also a Burgess Shale display at the picnic area. From this lake, you can see in the mountains above, the Burgess Shale, one of the richest finds of fossils in the world.

Takakkaw Falls – ½ day

Located 8 miles (13 kilometers) down Yoho Valley Road, at the East end of the valley in Yoho National Park, you will come to Takakkaw

Falls. Please note, that this road is not suitable for travel trailers or long vehicles. In fact, the switchbacks are so tight on this road, that the bus tours that come up the road, actually have to drive up one switchback, then reverse up the next, then drive the next and then reverse up the following one. It is a pretty scary road!

If you survive the switchbacks (just kidding), there is a large parking lot complete with picnic tables and public washrooms. The falls are visible from the road and the parking lot, but you can walk a short trail to the base of the falls if you so choose. It is an easy trail, climbing only gradually as you near the base of the falls. You will get pretty wet though if you go all the way to the base of the falls. In summer, this is a very refreshing walk.

The name Takakkaw means "magnificent" in Cree, and it is a very appropriate word to describe these falls. They are the second highest falls in Canada, as they plunge from a height of 1246 feet (380 meters) with a free fall of 833 feet (254 meters). If you have the time for a side trip, these falls are worth the drive.

Lake O'Hara – 1 day

The Lake O'Hara parking lot is located 7.5 miles (12 kilometers) west of Lake Louise, about ten minutes drive. This is a restricted lake in that you cannot drive into it, but either have to reserve a place on a bus or hike 6.8 miles (11 kilometers) to the lake one way. Parks Canada recommends reserving your place on the bus, one full year in advance. This is a beautiful lake in a magnificent setting, but a lot of work to get to. Most of the trail is uphill. There is a resort located on the lake and you can make reservations to stay at the resort. Unless you have a bus reservation or are a sturdy hiker, I would give this one a miss.

For more information on Lake O'Hara, please view the Parks Canada website.

Burgess Shale

The Burgess Shale Formation is one of the most celebrated fossil beds in the world. Located high on a mountain, to the west of Lake Louise in the Yoho Valley, the Burgess Shale is a protected area. You will need to book a guide to visit the formation, and the tours are very limited. The shale beds hosts one of the richest fossil beds the world has come across.

It was discovered in 1909 by Charles Doolittle Walcott and since been protected by Parks Canada and UNESCO. The Burgess Shale is now a recognized as a World Heritage Site.

You can book a tour of the Burgess Shale through Parks Canada.

Chapter Eleven – Bow Valley Parkway – ½ day to 1 day

The Bow Valley Parkway, Highway 1A, is a secondary Highway that runs between Lake Louise and Banff. If you want to take a slower route and enjoy the scenery more, then this is the route to take. You will also have a much better chance of spotting wildlife on this quieter back road.

Bow Valley Parkway – ½ day

You can access the Bow Valley Parkway (Highway 1A) from three different places, Lake Louise, Banff and Castle Junction (where Highway 1 intersects Highway 93). Your best bet is to get on to it at either Lake Louise or Banff.

The speed limit on the Bow Valley Parkway is 37 MPH (60 KMH) and there are travel restrictions on the road at certain times of the year for a few hours each night. Check with Parks Canada for more details about closures and restrictions.

This scenic route was actually Highway 1 (Trans Canada Highway) before the highway was moved to its current location. Because you are traveling at a slower pace, you will have the opportunity to take in more of the views and the wildlife. On top of this, Parks Canada has set up 11 interpretative signs along the highway to explain the interesting features, flowers, or wildlife at the various stops.

If you have a half-day to spend on this road, it will be well worth it. There are far more opportunities to view things than there is on the Trans Canada Highway, which is a very busy highway. So busy in fact, that Parks Canada have fenced it off and built walkways for animals to cross the highway and go under it.

The highlights of this trip will be Castle Mountain, a fantastic looking mountain that resembles a castle, which there is a pullover and an observation platform for taking photographs. The other highlight will be Johnston Canyon.

Johnston Canyon – 1 hour to ½ day

Johnston Canyon is located about ½ hour from Banff on Highway 1A. It is close to Castle Junction, where Highway 1 meets Highway 93. If it is one of the times where Highway 1A is closed, you can use Highway 1 to access Johnston Canyon.

At this location, you will find a large parking lot, a resort, restaurant, souvenir shop and an ice cream shop. You will also find a paved trail that goes into the canyon. There are three different destinations in this canyon, each one further than the last. The trail through the canyon is paved to the Lower Falls, easily accessible, climbs a little and at times, you are actually on catwalks that are attached to the side of the canyon – very thrilling!

The first destination is the Lower Falls, which are 0.68 of a mile (1.1 kilometers) from the trailhead. It should take about 20 minutes one way to walk to these falls. You won't be disappointed, the falls come into a bowl and there is a viewing area here. Over time, the falls had carved a tunnel through the rock face and since abandoned. You can now go into the tunnel and look out the other end to see the falls.

The second destination is the Upper Falls, which are 1.7 miles (2.7 kilometers) from the trailhead. It should take about an hour one-way to reach the falls. The trail here is no longer paved and a little more rugged. These falls are higher than the Lower Falls and you can hike around them to the top of them. The drop on these falls is almost 100 feet (30 meters).

The third destination is the Ink Pots, which are 3.7 miles (5.9 kilometers) from the trailhead. I cannot accurately give you an estimate of the time required to hike to the Ink Pots, which depends upon your own level of fitness. Parks Canada lists this as an easy to moderate hike requiring about 4 to 5 hours for the return trip. While the terrain is not challenging at all, it is a constant up hill climb to reach the Ink Pots. Suffice to say, the return journey is a lot easier. If you choose to hike to the Ink Pots, you will not be disappointed! When you reach the end of the trail (which is well marked, wide and well maintained), you will be in an open meadow surrounded by mountains on all sides. That alone is worth the trip, to be surrounded by mountains, with no sign of human structures, roads or towers, just unspoiled beauty is one of the rewards for the hike. The other reward is the Ink Pots; these are pools of bubbling water, with deep hues of green, blue, and purple in the water, caused by minerals in the rocks below. Unfortunately they are very difficult to photograph and the color rarely shows in a picture. There are benches here so you can rest and enjoy a picnic. There are no washrooms; in fact, the closest ones are at the trailhead.

Johnston Canyon is a very busy place, particularly the trail to the Lower and Upper Falls. After you pass the Upper Falls, the crowds thin out. If you were planning on doing the Ink Pots, I would recommend an early start. Also, as the day progresses, the parking lot becomes fuller. On one of our visits, we were forced to park illegally on Highway 1A. Johnston Canyon is one of the most unique walks you will do in the Canadian Rockies, but also one of the busiest. Note, that it is very cool inside the canyon, so bring something warm to wear, even in summer.

Chapter Twelve – Banff – 2 to 3 days

The town of Banff is located just off Highway 1 (Trans Canada Highway), 80 miles (128 kilometers) east of Calgary, Alberta and 526 miles (847 kilometers) west of Vancouver, BC. Banff is the largest of the towns located in the Rocky Mountain Parks of Jasper, Banff and Yoho. Banff has all the amenities of a modern town, including fuel, banks, grocery stores, retail stores, restaurants, pubs and anything else you can think of. Actually there is one thing that cannot be found here (as of 2011) and it astounds me, you cannot get a propane bottle filled! You have to either go to Lake Louise to the west or Canmore to the east. Actually, I have been unable to find any free Wifi here as well, even though many websites claim it exists. There is an Internet cafe on the main street in a downstairs mall. There are two different places to do laundry in Banff.

Banff also has a public transit system as well, which at one time used to visit all of the Tunnel Mountain campgrounds. I believe now it only comes to the one closest to town, you will need to check with Parks Canada or the Town of Banff website for more information on transit. *http://www.banff.ca/*

Banff is a wonderful place to walk around; it is amazing to find a town of this size located in such a beautiful place. There are many shops along the main street and some of the back avenues as well. I mentioned earlier on in this book, that the souvenir shops mostly cater to the Asian market, which means finding an authentic souvenir of Banff, other than a t-shirt, is getting harder all the time.

There are many campgrounds run by Parks Canada in Banff, Tunnel Mountain I, II, and III being the closest to town, which each one offers different services. One of the Tunnel Mountain campgrounds is actually a trailer court and there is no overnight camping, that is the closest to Banff, and the one that has public transit coming to it. The next one is Tunnel Mountain II, which has power at all of the campsites, but no fire pits. The final one is Tunnel Mountain III, which is a wilderness campground with no power, but has fire pits. Further out, on the North side of the Trans Canada Highway, there are two more campsites called Two Jacks, which are a little more rugged than the Tunnel Mountain ones. We usually stay at Tunnel

Mountain II or III because of the transit. It is nice to be able to take the bus into town and enjoy one of the local pubs, particularly if it is a rainy day.

Within the actual town site of Banff, there are quite a few things to see, other than the town itself; these include the Banff Park Museum, the Whyte Museum, and the Cascade Gardens at the Park Administration Building. As you cross the Bow River, you will find the Cave & Basin National Historic Site, The Banff Springs Hotel, Bow Falls, and the Banff Gondola. Following the road that goes around Tunnel Mountain (Tunnel Mountain Drive), you will find the other look out for Bow Falls that offers a fantastic view of the Banff Springs Hotel. As well as the trailhead for climbing Tunnel Mountain – a nice hike, that is worth the effort. As you continue on Tunnel Mountain Drive, it goes around Tunnel Mountain and you find yourself back on Tunnel Mountain Road, where the campgrounds are located. This road has a rest stop where the Hoodoos are located. If you continue on this road, you will eventually meet up with Banff Avenue, the main thoroughfare of Banff. Take this road across Highway 1 (Trans Canada Highway) and there are more sites to see such as Cascade Ponds, Bankhead and Lake Minnewanka. This road is actually a loop and makes a nice drive, which brings you right back to where you started, at Highway 1. Everything around Banff is very close to town, with the exception of the Minnewanka Loop. Everything else can be found within 10 minutes of the downtown core.

Town of Banff – ½ day to 1 day

I've already mentioned a lot about the town of Banff. One could spend an entire day here, just walking around the shops. There's even a candy shop, which is a ½ hour alone to go through everything. You'll also find a homemade fudge store, as well as many, many souvenir shops. There are several pubs and restaurants to enjoy as well. Near the Bow River is a park with picnic tables if you wish to enjoy a picnic. Apart from all the man made stuff, you can find plenty of walking trails around Banff. Parks Canada also maintains a visitor center here, where you can learn more information about the conditions of local trails, attractions and closures.

On many of the buildings in Banff, you will find a plaque and picture with a story. The historical significance of many of the buildings is told on these plaques.

Banff Park Museum – 1 to 2 hours

The Banff Park Museum is a National Historic site located near the Bow River on Banff Avenue. It is a very unique building as it was designed to take advantage of natural light to light the interior. It was built in 1903 and was a showpiece of Banff National Park. One would expect that this building be filled with local specimens from within the mountain parks; however, it actually contains over 5000 species of plants and animals from around the world. It did originally start out as only specimens from the parks, but grew with time and the changing attitudes of the administration.

Whyte Museum – 1 to 2 hours

Opened in 1968, the Whyte Museum is actually an art gallery showing off contemporary artists renderings of the surrounding mountains and scenery. To learn more about the Whyte Museum, you can check their website to see what is currently showing: *http://www.whyte.org*

Cascade Gardens at the Park Administration Building – 1 hour or more

Across the Bow River, at the end of Banff Avenue, is a building that towers over the landscape, almost looking like a castle. It is surrounded by a large wrought iron fence and looks like a very private place. It is the Administration Building for Parks Canada that was built in 1936 and was the first official representation of the Canadian Government in a National Park. Walk up to the front gate and open the gate; it is open to the public. Off to the right of the main building, you will find the Cascades of Time Gardens. The idea was to present a journey through time via a representation of the geological times in the Rockies using water and flowers. It was designed in 1934 and unfortunately, due to funding and other issues, never lived up to its designer's dreams. The ponds are no longer filled with water, as they require too much maintenance, however, the flowers are still here and are maintained annually. Enjoy a walk through this garden, where every flower, bush and tree is identified with a plaque.

Cave and Basin National Historic Site – 1 hour

Located across the Bow River on Cave Avenue, is the Cave and Basin National Historic site, which can be found at the end of Cave Avenue. There is a large parking lot for visitors. This used to be the actual hot springs that the tourists all came to see and enjoy. The site is now a museum and you can go into the cave, where the original hot springs were found. This is actually the birthplace of Banff and Banff National Park. There is also a pool outside the main building that you may have seen in old photographs of Banff National Park. The old hot pool for the public is now a reflection pond in the main building. To enjoy a hot spring in Banff, you can go to the public pools at Sulphur Mountain, down the road a bit on Spray Avenue.

Banff Gondola – 2 hours

The advertising for the Banff Gondola says it is the best thing to do in Banff National Park, and I think I have to agree with them, well for the most part. This is a great ride to the top of Sulphur Mountain; you can see the town of Banff below, the Banff Springs Hotel and the Bow Valley. In the distance is Lake Minnewanka. The gondola ascends 2292 feet (698 meters) to reach an altitude of 7486 feet (2281 meters). Once at the top, you follow a boardwalk to the old weather observatory. From here, you have an unobstructed 360 degree view of the valleys below. The hours of operation and the prices for admission can be found on the Banff Gondola's website *http://www.explorerockies.com/banff-gondola/*

If you are going to Banff and the weather is good, then do not miss this attraction! Here's a little tip, often this ride is combined with other attractions in the Rockies and you can get a discount ticket for two or more attractions, often these coupons are found on the website, or in the brochures handed out at most souvenir shops.

For the unmatched views of the Rockies, I would rate this as one of the top ten best things to see or do in the Canadian Rockies.

Banff Springs Hotel – 1 hour

The Banff Springs Hotel is truly a castle in the Rockies! It was built by the Canadian Pacific Railway to attract tourists to their new railway line in the late 1800's. It is now run by Fairmont Hotels, the same as the Chateau Lake Louise. The Banff Springs Hotel is styled after a Scottish Baronial Castle. The site is now a National Historic Site of Canada. The hotel is located on Spray Avenue, to get here, follow Banff Avenue across the Bow River and then turn left. Follow the road until you come across the parking lot for the hotel. Note, it is pay parking here, so you may want to park on the road (if you can find a spot) before you reach the hotel property.

The Banff Springs hotel is not as open to the public as the Chateau Lake Louise is. You can enter the main entrance; there is an area just up stairs in the main lobby that has pictures and stories of the history of the hotel. You can usually view the formal dining room and the tearoom. You can also eat at one of the restaurants. There is a small area downstairs with some stores that the public may visit. Most areas of the hotel are restricted to guests. The outside however, you can pretty much walk anywhere. Often in summer, you will find a Royal Canadian Mounted Police officer in full dress uniform with his or her horse. You may, with the officers permission have your picture taken with a real Mountie.

Bow Falls – 1 hour

Bow Falls are located behind the Banff Springs Hotel. You access them via Spray Avenue and then turn left onto Rundle Avenue, then right onto Bow River Avenue. It is well posted (as with most attractions in the Canadian Rockies). Once there, you will find a large parking lot. From the parking lot, there are washrooms and benches to sit on. Close to where you park, on the right, the Spray River meets the Bow River. You will often see whitewater rafts in this area. To your left you will see the small canyon that the Bow River Falls go through. They look like a series of slides coming through the canyon. There are some steps here that you can take and follow the river and see more of the rapids and falls. The trail actually leads back to town and one can walk from town to this spot.

Tunnel Mountain – 1 to 3 hours

Right in the middle of Banff, there is a mountain that looks like a buffalo. It is called Tunnel Mountain. It stands at 5544 feet (1690 meters) and by Rockies standards is more of a foothill than a mountain. Around Tunnel Mountain, on Tunnel Mountain Drive are several viewpoints where you can take in some of the scenery. Some of them have parking lots and some are just pull offs. They are all well posted and easy to find. One of the viewpoints overlooks the golf course and the Bow River. Another viewpoint gives you a nice view of the Bow Falls. Above this viewpoint, is another viewpoint that is a wooden walkway. There are information signs here about the Douglas Fir trees and it is an excellent place to take a photograph of the Banff Springs Hotel.

About midway along Tunnel Mountain Drive is a pull off with some parking spots; usually all full during the day, but in the early morning are usually available. Right across the street from these parking spots, is the trailhead for Tunnel Mountain. It is well marked. The trail for Tunnel Mountain weaves back and forth across the front of the mountain and is a 2.86 mile (4.6 kilometer) round trip hike, which climbs 984 feet (300 meters). It takes roughly 2 to 3 hours depending upon your physical condition. If there is anything you are going to do in Banff, particularly if you didn't go up the gondola, take this hike. The view from here is fantastic. Not only that, though, as you near the top, the trail actually goes to the back side of the mountain and you have a fantastic view of Lake Minnewanka, the Tunnel Mountain campgrounds, the golf course and on towards Canmore. When you reach the top, you have a view of the town of Banff, as well as the entire valley towards Lake Louise.

Hoodoos – ½ hour

Located right near the Tunnel Mountain campgrounds is a parking lot for the trailhead to the Hoodoos. The trail is very short and it is all level. A short distance from the parking lot will bring you to the Hoodoos. More Hoodoos can also be spotted from Highway 1 (Trans Canada Highway) near the TransAlta power plant as you are heading towards Canmore from Banff.

Cascade Ponds – 1 hour

Follow Banff Avenue towards the Trans Canada Highway. On the north side of the highway, the road turns into Lake Minnewanka Scenic Drive. A short distance from the Trans Canada Highway, on your right hand side will be a short gravel road that leads to a parking lot. This is the parking lot for Cascade Ponds. Cascade Ponds are a group of small ponds that you can walk around and relax. There are some bridges that take the trail onto a small island. From here you have a great view of Cascade Mountain towering over you. There are picnic tables and washrooms here. It is a great place to relax, and is treasured by locals and visitors alike.

Bankhead – ½ hour

Further down the Lake Minnewanka Scenic Drive is the parking lot for Bankhead. Bankhead was an old community that once existed here, before Banff became a National Park. There was a lot of coal mining in the area and the remnants of the old coal mine and equipment can be found via this short hike. Many of the houses that once existed here, were actually moved to the town of Banff. If you are walking around Banff, you will come across some of the houses that were moved, they have plaques in front of them to indicate their historic significance.

The self-guided interpretative trail is .68 of a mile (1.1 kilometers) and will take about 30 minutes to walk around.

Lake Minnewanka – 1 to 3 hours

A little further down the road from Bankhead, you will find Lake Minnewanka, a pretty turquoise lake with boat tours on it. It is actually a man made lake, with a dam on the south end of it, where you come into it. There is a large parking lot here, where you can get out and walk the shoreline. For the more experienced hikers, you can hike quite a distance here and spend the night in several backcountry campgrounds. For the less adventurous, there is a nice ice cream shop here, have a cone and enjoy the scenery. As I mentioned, you can also take a boat tour here. Lake Minnewanka is one of two lakes in the Rocky Mountain Parks that allow motorized boats on them, the other being Maligne Lake, near Jasper. The boat tour lasts about one hour. For more information on book a boat tour, please check out the website for

http://www.explorerockies.com/minnewanka/

This is one of the attractions that is sometimes bundled with the Banff Gondola, so check the website and local brochures for deals.

There is actually an old town buried beneath the water of Lake Minnewanka, there are interpretative signs along the lake to let you know more about the history.

Minnewanka Loop – ½ hour to 1 hour

If you have reached Lake Minnewanka, you can then cross the end of the lake, on Minnewanka Loop. This drive continues on past Two Jack Lake, the Two Jack Campgrounds and Johnson Lake, before returning back to Lake Minnewanka Scenic Drive. It is a nice drive that takes you to some small lakes, mostly to do with hydroelectric activities. Each lake has an interpretative sign to tell you a little bit about the history.

Conclusion

I hope this book has been helpful to you in planning your next trip to the Canadian Rockies. After telling so many tourists about the Canadian Rockies, I figured it was time to write about it so that many others could benefit from my knowledge.

I have enjoyed writing this book, as much as I enjoy telling visitors about the wonderful places to visit in the Rockies. I still to this day continue to visit the Canadian Rockies and find new things to see and do.

If you are in an RV and taking Highway 1 (The Trans Canada Highway) to or from the Canadian Rockies, then may I suggest you stop at one of my favorite campsites, Noah's Ark Resort (*www.noahsarkresort.com*) in Revelstoke, British Columbia. It is where the idea for this book was born.

If you have any questions or comments, you can contact me through my website: *http://www.darrencritchley.com/*

If you enjoyed this book, then please let your friends know or give the book a review on Amazon.

Darren

Darren Critchley

541 963 3707

Sandman

Craig
206 384 1924

Made in the USA
San Bernardino, CA
02 July 2014